Bite-Sized Science

Bite-Sized Science

Activities for Children in 15 Minutes or Less

John H. Falk and Kristi S. Rosenberg

CHICAGO REVIEW PRESS

Library of Congress Cataloging-in-Publication Data

Falk, John H. (John Howard), 1948–
    Bite-sized science : activities for children in 15 minutes or less/
    John H. Falk and Kristi S. Rosenberg. — 1st ed.
        p. cm.
    ISBN 1-55652-348-3
    1. Science—Study and teaching (Preschool)—Activity programs.
2. Education, Preschool—Activity programs. I. Rosenberg, Kristi S. II. Title.
LB1140.5.S35F35   1999
372.3'5044—dc21   98–49814
                                                                             CIP

The author and the publisher of this book disclaim all liability incurred in connection with the use of the information contained in this book.

Cover and interior illustrations: © Bonnie Matthews
Cover and interior design: Mel Kupfer

First edition
Published by Chicago Review Press, Incorporated
814 North Franklin Street
Chicago, Illinois 60610
ISBN 978-1-55652-348-9
Printed in the United States of America
10 9 8 7

For the parents and children
who tested these activities
and for Robert Pruitt
for his guidance and enthusiasm

Contents

Introduction   ix

1

In the Kitchen   1

Cupboard Talk   2

Foil Molds   4

Hear It Again   6

How Many Seeds?   9

Clinks in the Kitchen   12

So Much Popcorn!   14

Soften It   17

Chewing Sounds   19

Tangy Tongue   21

2

High Energy   25

Bridge It   26

Eye Can Catch It, Maybe   29

Flex Those Muscles   31

Floor Textures   32

Light Weight   35

Look, No Hands!   38

Shoebox Sounds   40

Toss It!   42

Walk This Way   44

What Makes a Foot?   48

3

Quiet Times 51

Can You Hear It? 52

Hidden Message 54

How Much Can You See? 56

Magnify It 59

Mirror Images 61

Mirror Me 63

Shoe Show 65

Tea Time 68

Tooth Talk 71

What Color Is It? 73

Without a Sound 75

4

Bedtime 77

One, Two, Pick Up My Room 78

Making Waves 80

Shower Sounds 83

Water Levels 85

What's on the Wall? 87

5

Bigger than a Bite 89

Hot Sweaty Trees 90

Let the Sun Shine In 93

Pet Play 96

Pint-Sized Playground 99

Vanishing Colors 101

Bibliography 105

Acknowledgments 107

INTRODUCTION

Food for Thought

Children are so wonderful—bright, earnest, and ever curious—hungering for knowledge about their world. It is just these attributes that we seek to encourage and build upon in *Bite-Sized Science*. And it is the metaphor of hungering for knowledge that led us to the current approach and format for this book. This is a recipe book for learning, designed to help parents feed their young child's seemingly never-ending quest for understanding about the world.

Food and knowledge are hardly strange bedfellows—the two have been figuratively and literally intertwined for thousands of years. Just as a healthy, growing body requires the right kinds of foods, so too does a healthy, growing mind require the right kinds of information. *Bite-Sized Science* delivers healthy food for developing minds. The science in this book is not only nourishing and child appropriate but also deliciously fun. Picking up popcorn using just your tongue or sampling sweet- and sour-tasting sauces at supper to see how they tickle your tongue—what could be more fun for children ages three to eight? Each activity is both wonderfully fun and truly educational, teaching real science, the kind that helps young minds discover the wonders and workings of the natural world.

Despite its mystique and complex nature, science can be reduced to a few fundamental rules—rules that even a three-year-old can learn. Good science rests on three basic tenets—making predictions about the world, testing those predictions, and then evaluating the results against the original predictions. Every scientific experiment begins with a hypothesis: What do I think will happen if I do this? How many whatsits will it take to make this thingamajig work? Why do I think this happened now instead of something else? Once a hypothesis has been made, it can be tested to see if it works. Finally, when all the testing is over, it is important to go back to the original hypothesis and see if it was true. If yes, great, if not, we need to formulate a new hypothesis to better predict the outcome. This is the nature of science whether the subject of study is chemistry, physics, or biology. It's really not that complicated. Science is not really about facts and concepts, rather, it's a process of asking questions and attempting to systematically answer them. The activities in *Bite-Sized Science* are all built upon this premise. With the help of a willing and able parent, every child can become a scientist. In fact, with the help of a willing and able child, every parent can become a scientist too! As you use this book, we hope you'll remember this and

1. ask your child to make predictions,
2. do the activity, and
3. come back to those predictions again.

Follow these three steps every time, and this way of thinking will become habitual. In doing so, you will have played a major role in helping to create a future scientist. No matter what your child ends up doing in his or her life, being inquisitive and scientific in his or her thinking will prove invaluable and beneficial.

A Science Book Specially Designed for Parents

● ● ● ● ● ● ● ● ● ● ● ● ● ● ● ● ●

Bite-Sized Science is not your ordinary science activity book. It's been developed with busy parents in mind. Over the years we have been involved in developing a number of highly successful science activity books for children, including *Bubble Monster and Other Science Fun*. Many users of these materials, including parents, have complimented us on the fun and innovative activities that we have created for young children and their caretakers. However, the needs of parents and professional child-care providers differ in a number of important ways. For example, parents know their children very well, know their likes and dislikes, strengths and weaknesses better than any part-time caregiver or teacher. Also, parents aren't working with large numbers of same-aged children, but one, two, or three children, each of a different age and typically each with a very different set of interests and abilities. Finally, and perhaps most critically, parents often have only a limited amount of time to interact with their children. As parents ourselves, we understand these important realities, particularly the issue of time.

Finding quality time to do something meaningful with our children is challenging. *Bite-Sized Science* was developed to facilitate quality science learning opportunities for busy parents and their children. Each activity is designed to take only a few minutes to organize, initiate, conduct, and clean up, unless otherwise noted. Each activity is designed to fit seamlessly within the daily routines of families—activities like making meals, bath time, and those few extra moments before bedtime. We believe education is not something that just happens in a place called school; education is something every parent provides his or her child every day. Education, though, need not be limited in either its content or scope. We believe parents can directly help their children with every manner of learning, including science, if they have the appropriate tools at their disposal.

Each activity in the book is a self-contained recipe and includes a materials list for doing the science activity, the steps you'll need to follow, suggestions for other activities you can do later, and some background information about the topic presented. Remember to ask your child to develop a hypothesis.

We realize you may want more information. So, just as many cookbooks intersperse cooking tips throughout, we have scattered facts and tips throughout this book. Throughout the book is information on child development, tips on question asking and hypothesis generation, and even an occasional anecdote from someone who did one of activities at home with his or her child.

Bon appétit!

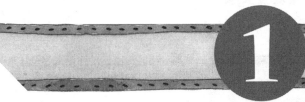

1

In the Kitchen

• •

Every home comes equipped with a science laboratory!
Try these activities while preparing meals or snacks
or when you just feel like messing around with science.

Cupboard Talk

What You Will Do

Take items from the cupboard and shake them while your child has his eyes closed. He will try to guess what food you are shaking.

Your Child

If your child is younger than five years old, select only two or three items and let him see the items before you shake them. If he does this well, try other items without showing them to him first.

Fact

Containers are made of different materials. The materials will either absorb or reflect sound. When you shake a container, it may make a sound. The container and what is inside will determine what type of sound is produced. A tin can makes soup sound sloshy or makes rice sound piercing. A cardboard box with rice in it will not be as loud as the tin can with rice in it.

What You Need

- ★ Several items from the cupboard, such as a can of soup, a box of rice, or salt and pepper containers

1. Select several items from the cupboard that will make a sound. Place them on the counter for your child to see. No shaking the items!

2. Ask him to close his eyes. Shake one of the items close to his ear. Can he guess which item you shook? If he's not sure, shake the item again.

3. Repeat step 2 until your child identifies all the items.

4. If he guesses them easily, select a few more items, but do not let him see them. Now, shake one of the items and ask him to guess what it is.

5. Let him select and shake some items for you to guess.

 My three-year-old really loved this activity. She made me do it over and over again.
—Mildred Pertz, Akron, Ohio

Foil Molds

What You Will Do

Using several pieces of aluminum foil, you and your child will make molds of items in the house and then try to identify each other's molds.

Your Child

If your child is younger than five years old, make molds of her toys. This will help her begin to recognize patterns. She may need help making the molds.

Fact

We recognize items by their patterns and shapes. We store certain patterns and shapes in our memory and can recall them when we see them. The molds you and your child make have certain patterns and shapes, and if you have seen the pattern or shape before, your memory will help you recall what item made the mold.

What You Need

★ **3 pieces aluminum foil of different sizes for each of you**
★ **Wrist watch or clock**

1. Give your child three pieces of aluminum foil and ask her to find items to mold in the foil, such as light switches, doorknobs, someone's nose, or an interesting shaped object. You have five minutes! (Keep time using the wrist watch or clock.)

2. The aluminum foil needs to be slightly bigger than the item you want to mold. Carefully place the foil around the item and mold the foil to the item with your hand. Carefully remove the foil. The edges of the foil may need to be loosened to remove the foil. Continue this process until each of you has three molds.

3. Now try to guess what item made each mold. Give each other hints if you need to.

4. Were you able to guess all of the molds? Was it difficult to identify what made the molds? Was it difficult because you were not familiar with the items?

Hear It Again

What You Will Do

Your child will create echoes using kitchen items made of different types of materials.

Your Child

If your child is between three and five, try steps 1 and 2 only, asking him to tell you when he hears a different sound.

Fact

Objects produce different echoes because of the materials they are made from. When sound hits them, some materials are more absorbent, and some are more reflective. The arrangement of the molecules within the materials determines whether sound is absorbed or reflected. If the molecules' bonds are strong, the sound is reflected. If the molecules' bonds are weak, the sound is absorbed. If the sound echoes loudly and you can hear it well, it is reflected. If the sound echoes softly or not at all, the sound is absorbed.

What You Need

★ Deep and wide pots
★ Metal or nonstick coated pans
★ Plates
★ Cookie sheets

6

1. Ask your child to help collect all of the items and place them on the counter. Ask him to close his eyes, take a deep breath, and hum loudly as you hold one of the items approximately 12 inches from his face.

2. Ask him to describe what he hears. You may need to move the item a little closer to his face. Also, try moving the item from left to right in front of your child's face so he will recognize the vibration or echo. Repeat steps 1 and 2 using different items.

3. Help your child decide which of the items produces the loudest, deepest, or longest echoes. Are any of these items made from the same materials?

4. Try grouping together items that make similar echoes. Do any of the materials have similar properties?

An Extra Bite

. . . .

A scavenger hunt! Collect other items from around the house and place them all on a table. Predict which items will make the loudest echoes and then listen to the echoes. Use the same method as described in step 1 above. Compare the results with the predictions that you made. What are the properties of the items that made the loudest echoes? Are they similar to each other?

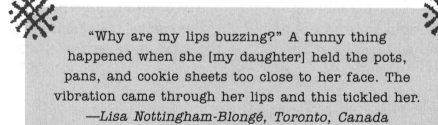

"Why are my lips buzzing?" A funny thing happened when she [my daughter] held the pots, pans, and cookie sheets too close to her face. The vibration came through her lips and this tickled her.
—*Lisa Nottingham-Blongé, Toronto, Canada*

How Many Seeds?

What You Will Do

While you are slicing fruits and vegetables for a snack or dinner, have your child predict how many seeds are in each piece.

Your Child

If your child is just learning to count, help her count the number of seeds she finds in each piece. Using fruits and vegetables that have few seeds would be a good place to start for young counters.

Fact

Prediction is at the heart of all science. We make predictions based on acquired knowledge and experiences. We use observation skills to test our predictions. As we test our predictions, we learn from them and are able to make predictions more accurately in the future.

9

What You Need

* ★ Cucumbers and peppers
  (or other fruits and vegetables
  containing seeds)
* ★ Knife

Play It Safe! Always exercise caution when using a knife around young children.

1. Make sure your child has clean hands before starting this activity.

2. Ask her to guess how many seeds will be in a slice of cucumber. Give her one slice at a time to count the number of seeds. Is there the same number of seeds in each slice?

3. Ask her to make a prediction of how many seeds are in a pepper. Cut the top off a pepper for her and scoop out the core and seeds. Now, have her count the seeds and compare the number with her prediction.

An Extra Bite

. . . .

Try planting the seeds! Take a little pot or a paper cup with a small hole in the bottom and fill it with soil. With your finger, poke a hole in the soil about a half inch deep and put a couple of seeds in it. Refill the hole. Keep the pot or cup in a sunny place and water when the soil gets dry. It may take a week or two to see anything grow, so be patient and encourage your child to take care of her growing seeds.

The world's largest cucumber weighed 21 pounds and 4½ ounces and was grown by P. Glazebrook from Nework, England in 1996.
The world's largest tomato weighed 7 pounds and 12 ounces and was grown by G. Graham from Edmond, Oklahoma, in 1986.

Clinks in the Kitchen

What You Will Do

Create sounds with different types of foods by dropping them into bowls made of different materials.

Fact

When you pour or drop food into a bowl, it makes a sound. The bowls are made of different materials, which means the molecules are bonding in different ways. Metal bowls have tight bonds, and plastic bowls have looser bonds. Dropping cereal into a metal bowl causes the molecules to vibrate and create a loud sound because the bonds are so tight that the sound just bounces off the bowl. A plastic bowl will make a softer sound because the molecules are loose and will absorb some of the sound and create less vibration.

What You Need

★ 1 metal bowl
★ 1 plastic bowl
★ 1 porcelain bowl
★ 1 china bowl
★ 1 ceramic bowl
★ Uncooked rice
★ Dry cereal
★ Uncooked pasta

1. Place three of the bowls and the food on the counter.

2. Ask your child to close his eyes.

3. Slowly drop the rice into one of the bowls.

4. With his eyes still closed, ask your child to guess which bowl the rice was dropped into.

5. If his guess is correct, try it with the remaining two bowls. If he needs another chance to guess, drop the rice into the same bowl again.

6. Keep dropping the different food items into the bowls and listen to the sounds that are made.

So Much Popcorn!

What You Will Do

Compare popcorn before and after it is popped. You will want to make the popcorn in a popcorn maker or in a pan on the stove. Microwave popcorn will not work for this activity.

Fact

Heated oil causes popcorn seeds to literally explode. When it explodes, the volume of the seed is enlarged. When your child compares the number of pieces of popped corn in a cup to the number of popcorn seeds in a cup, she will discover there are fewer pieces of popped corn than unpopped corn.

What You Need

* ★ Popcorn seeds
* ★ Measuring cup
* ★ Pencil
* ★ Plain white paper
* ★ Oil
* ★ Popcorn maker or pan with a lid

Play It Safe! Allow your child to help make the popcorn on the stove, but she should not do this alone.

1. Help your child pour the popcorn seeds into a measuring cup. Ask her to guess how many seeds are in the cup. Write her answer on the piece of paper.

2. Now have her count the number of seeds in the cup. Record this number.

3. Help your child pour a small amount of oil in the popcorn maker or pan and then add the popcorn seeds. Turn on the stove and shake the pot occasionally as the seeds cook. While you are waiting for the popcorn to pop, ask your child how many pieces of popped popcorn will fit in the measuring cup. Record this number on the paper. Is her guess the same, higher, or lower than the number of seeds that were actually in the cup? Why did she make this guess?

4. After the popcorn has popped, ask your child to scoop out a measuring cup full of popcorn. Then, ask her to count the number of pieces of popcorn not including any unpopped seeds. How does this number compare with her guess? Is it different? Why is it different?

The world's largest popcorn ball was created by the Boy Scouts of America of the Gateway Area Council (LaCrosse, Wisconsin) in September 1995. The popcorn ball weighed 2,377 pounds and was 7 feet and 7 inches tall.

Soften It

What You Will Do

Put uncooked pasta or rice in a bowl of hot water and a bowl of cold water. This is a good activity to do before dinner, especially when you are making spaghetti, pasta, or rice dishes.

Fact

Most foods will absorb water, which causes them to become soft. Both pasta and rice are hard before they are placed in water. The temperature of the water will affect how quickly the pasta or rice softens. Warm water causes the molecules to move quickly and loosen faster than cold water.

What You Need

★ 2 bowls that will each hold 2 cups of water
★ 2 cups of hot water
★ 2 cups of cold water
★ Spoon
★ 2 spoonfuls of uncooked pasta or rice

Play It Safe! Always use caution when using hot water around young children.

1. Give your child one piece of pasta or rice. Ask him to feel it or try to break it. Is it difficult to break?

2. Place the bowls on the counter. Pour two cups of hot water in one bowl and ask your child to pour two cups of cold water in the other bowl.

17

3. Now, have him drop a spoonful of pasta or rice into each bowl. (Make sure there are at least five pieces in each bowl.) Ask him which bowl of water he thinks will soften the pasta or rice more quickly.

4. Wait two minutes. Ask him to scoop out one piece or pasta or rice from each bowl. Ask him to feel the pasta or rice from each bowl and try pressing a finger-nail into each. Is there a difference between the two pieces? How are the pieces different?

5. After another two minutes, scoop out another piece from each bowl. Compare them to the first two pieces. Do they feel different or the same? Have your child predict how the pasta or rice will feel in another two minutes.

Never tell people *how* to do things. Tell them *what* to do and they will surprise you with their ingenuity.
—*George S. Patton*

Chewing Sounds

What You Will Do

Your child will chew several different foods and listen to the way they sound. She will also chew the foods with her ears plugged. This activity can be done during dinner with the understanding that the child is doing an activity and should only do this at home with permission.

Fact

The foods we chew sound different depending on what they are made of and how they are heard. Soft foods may make squishing sounds or no sounds at all. Hard foods may make crunching or snapping sounds. We can hear the sounds we make when we chew, and we can hear the sounds other people make when they chew. If we plug our ears and chew, we hear different sounds too. For example, we may hear our teeth hitting each other or our jaw moving up and down, or we may hear swallowing. When we plug our ears we can hear sounds coming from inside our bodies because we have blocked out louder competing sounds coming from outside.

What You Need

★ 3 soft foods, such as bread, bananas, and cheese
★ 3 hard foods, such as crackers, raw carrots, and dry cereal

19

1. Ask your child to choose one of the six foods and chew it. Have her listen to the sound she hears.

2. Ask her if she thinks the sound will be louder or softer if she plugs her ears. Have her plug her ears and listen to what she hears.

3. Now it is your child's turn to listen to you chew the same food. Does it sound the same to her as it did when she was chewing? Is it a louder or softer sound?

4. Try the other foods. Do all foods make a sound when you chew? Can you guess what food each of you is chewing by the sound you hear?

An Extra Bite

Tape-record your child chewing and then play back the sounds. Can she tell which food she is chewing when the tape recorder plays the sound? Have her try creating sounds for foods that do not make any sounds, such as pudding or ice cream.

Tangy Tongue

What You Will Do

You and your whole family will taste several different seasonings or sauces and decide which ones you prefer. Try this activity when you are planning to make chicken for dinner. If your family is vegetarian, try different types of salad dressings or a variety of herbs and seasonings on pasta or rice.

SPICES AND SAUCES

Your Child

For children ages three to five, you may want to give them taste samples of sweet and sour so they have an idea of how they taste. You can also simply ask them which flavor chicken (or pasta or rice) they like the best and help them describe the flavor by asking questions about the seasoning or sauce.

Fact

We all have taste buds on our tongue, but we all have different taste preferences. Taste is like our other senses as far as what pleases us. Some people like the color blue while others like red. With taste, some people like sweet more than sour. While our tongue can tell us which flavor a food is, we determine whether we like the flavor based on our preference and past experience.

What You Need

★ Cooked chicken (or pasta or rice)
★ Several different seasonings or sauces, so each person will have a different one
★ Fork, knife, and plate for each person

1. Prepare the chicken without any seasonings.

2. Give all members of your family a piece of cooked chicken and have them cut it into several pieces, enough for each seasoning. Have them select a seasoning and lightly sprinkle it on one piece of chicken. Do they like it? Which type of seasoning did they have—sweet, sour, or bitter?

3. Ask them to exchange seasonings with the person next to them and repeat step 2 until everyone has tried each seasoning. Which seasoning did your family prefer? Is there one seasoning that everyone liked or disliked?

An Extra Bite

Explore cookbooks for recipes from different parts of the country. What foods do people from different parts of the country eat? Does their diet correlate with the agricultural sources or the environment of the area?

Explore cookbooks from around the world. Be adventurous and try many different seasonings.

 This activity was a real pleasure for the family or *mucho gusto* as we would say in Mexico. —Lupito Alverez, Austin, Texas

High Energy

Families, start your engines! Engage your
energetic child with these lively activities.

Bridge It

What You Will Do

Using pieces of cardboard and paper cups, your child will walk across a room to a designated spot without his feet touching the floor.

Your Child

If your child is under age five, he may not completely understand the concepts involved in this activity, but he will begin to develop building skills. He will also enjoy participating in a family or group activity.

Fact

Bridges allow us to get from one place to another while crossing over something else, such as a river. Bridges can

be made using different types of supports. The supports carry the weight of whatever is crossing the bridge. With the bridge that you build, paper cups support your child as he walks across the bridge. Each paper cup supports some of his weight. Your child is challenged to balance his weight as he walks from one cardboard platform to another. When he steps, his weight is initially on one foot and then on two feet as he completes his step. The placement of the cups plays an important part in the bridge being able to support him without collapsing.

What You Need

* ★ 100 medium-sized paper cups
* ★ 2 pieces of sturdy cardboard at least 12 by 12 inches
* ★ Tennis shoes or other shoes that will not slip on cardboard

Play It Safe! *Don't* let your child stand on the cardboard in just his socks. It is very slippery!

1. Together, choose the starting and ending points for your bridge. Make it a short distance at first.

 The longest bicycle/pedestrian bridge listed in the *Guinness Book of World Records* is the Old Chain of Rocks Bridge in Madison, Illinois. It is 5,350 feet long.

2. Ask your child to determine which way to place the paper cups on the floor (open end up or down) and in what design (in rows or some shape).

3. Ask him to arrange the paper cups on the floor and set one piece of cardboard on top of the cups. Help him step up on the cardboard and stand very still. Does the bridge hold him? If not, try again. If it did hold him, continue with step 4.

4. Remove any cups from under the platform that are not supporting any of your child's weight. These cups should come out easily.

5. Place the cups you removed in front of the platform your child is standing on, adding additional cups as needed.

Do not use any cups that are even slightly crushed. Place the other piece of cardboard on top of these cups.

6. Ask your child to carefully step to the next platform. You will continue moving the cups and two pieces of cardboard until your child has reached the designated place in the room.

An Extra Bite

Try switching places. Can he build a bridge to support you? What differences are there in the way the bridge is constructed? Are more cups needed when mom or dad stands on the bridge? After you have completed this activity be sure to recycle the paper cups and cardboard!

Eye Can Catch It, Maybe

Ages 5 to 7

What You Will Do

Play catch with your child while her eyes are open and then with one eye closed. She will discover she needs both of her eyes.

Your Child

Your child may have trouble closing just one eye. Fold a scarf or bandanna and gently tie it around your child's head so it covers one eye. You should also take a turn trying to catch with one eye closed. If your child sees that you too have trouble catching, she will not feel frustrated.

Fact

Our eyes allow us to see the world around us. They work together, but each sees an object from a different angle. Working together our eyes allow us to see depth. When only one eye is used to see, we lose depth perception. This means it is difficult for us to determine how far away or how close something is to us.

What You Need

· ·

★ Ball
★ Scarf or bandanna (optional)

1. Ask your child to stand about 10 feet away from you with her eyes open.

2. Toss the ball back and forth to each other.

3. When she has thrown and caught the ball several times, ask her to close her right eye, keep her head straight and looking forward, and continue to toss the ball. How is she doing? Ask her if she can see how close the ball is to her or if she is having trouble determining when the ball will reach her.

4. Now, have her open her eye again and toss the ball a few more times.

5. Ask her to close her left eye this time. What happens? Is it difficult for her to catch the ball? Can she catch better with both eyes open or with one closed?

Many of life's failures are people who did not realize how close they were to success when they gave up.
—*Thomas Edison*

Flex Those Muscles

What You Will Do

Make different facial expressions and feel the muscles moving.

Fact

Simple muscle contractions create movement. Sometimes the contractions move bones to allow us to walk or run. Other times the movement of muscles creates expressions on our face. We can flex the muscles above our eyes to raise our eyebrows to show surprise or to squint our eyes to show anger.

What You Need

★ Mirror

1. Ask your child to look in the mirror without making any facial expression. Have him place his hands on his face. Does he feel any muscles? Are any muscles working?

2. Now ask him to remove his hands and smile. Does he notice anything different about his face when he looks in the mirror?

3. Ask him to touch his face and smile. Can he feel anything different?

4. Have him try other facial expressions and feel the muscles moving.

5. Have him flex other muscles, such as his biceps and his calves. Can he feel the muscles contracting?

Floor Textures

What You Will Do

Your child will try to slide, in her socks, across different surfaces around the house.

Fact

The floors in your house are made of different materials. When another material slides across the surface of a floor, the resistance and heat created are caused by friction. Some materials create more friction than others. Depending on the type of floor material and the object sliding across it, you may see different reactions. For example, a smooth surface and a smooth item will have less friction and result in a faster slide while a rough surface and a rough item may result in a slow slide or no slide at all.

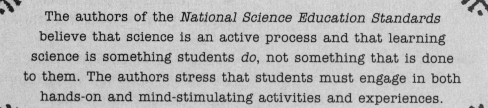

The authors of the *National Science Education Standards* believe that science is an active process and that learning science is something students *do*, not something that is done to them. The authors stress that students must engage in both hands-on and mind-stimulating activities and experiences.

What You Need

★ Socks
★ Different types of floor surfaces

Play It Safe! Since your child will be sliding across different surfaces, make sure there are no splinters in a wooden floor and the area is clear so she will not hit her toes or other body parts on any furniture. The first slide should be done slowly so your child will not fall. Once she is familiar with the surface, she may try the slide again.

1. Have your child put on a pair of socks.

2. Now, go through the house together and identify different floor textures, such as carpet, vinyl, tile, or wood. Which surfaces does she think will be easy to slide across in her socks?

3. Ask her to slide across one of the surfaces. What happened? Could she slide across the surface?

4. Try all of the surfaces in the house. What would make it easier to slide across the different surfaces?

Light Weight

What You Will Do

Standing on a chair, your child will drop a lightweight object into a box on the floor.

Your Child

If your child is under age five, ask him to hold an object in each hand and make observations about the objects. Ask him which object is heavier or lighter or which one will reach the floor faster if dropped.

Fact

Gravity is the force that causes an object to fall to the earth. The force of gravity pulls equally on all objects, regardless of weight, but other factors can affect the speed with which an object falls. In this activity, for example, air affects how the objects fall. If this experiment were conducted in a vacuum tube with all of the air sucked out, all the objects would fall at exactly the same speed.

What You Need

★ Small piece of paper
★ Cotton ball
★ Small piece of aluminum foil
★ Leaf
★ Toy or ball small enough to fit in the shoebox
★ Chair
★ Shoebox
★ Red crayon or marker

The Apollo 15 flight commander Dave Scott tested Galileo's theory that in the absence of air, all objects will fall at the same speed. On the moon, where there is no air, Scott dropped a hammer and a feather at the same time. They landed at the same time, proving Galileo was correct.

1. Ask your child to help you collect the items you need and put them on a table near the chair.

2. Ask him to draw a bull's-eye in the bottom of the shoebox with the red crayon.

3. Which items does he think will make it into the box?

4. Help him get up on the chair. Be sure to spot him while he stands on the chair. Ask him to hold his arm straight out in front of him. Place the shoebox on the floor directly under his hand.

5. Give him the items he collected and ask him to drop them one at a time into the box, trying to hit the bull's-eye. Did they all make it into the box? Which ones did not make it? What can he do to the items to make it easier to get them in the box?

6. Have him drop the toy or ball. How did this item fall compared to the others? Was it faster or slower? Did it hit the target?

Look, No Hands!

What You Will Do

Your child will try to eat popcorn and other favorite snacks without using her hands. You may want to use this activity in conjunction with the So Much Popcorn! activity (see Chapter 1). This activity is not a good example of proper table manners so explain to your child that this activity should only be done at home!

Fact

Popcorn is a snack food that we eat with our hands, no forks required. What happens when no hands are allowed? Our other options for getting the popcorn to our mouth are limited. We utilize other body parts to do what our hands cannot, and some work better than others or are more appropriate. Using your feet to eat may not be appropriate!

What You Need
. . . .

- ★ Popcorn without butter
- ★ Bowl
- ★ Snack foods, such as chips, pretzels, or crackers

Play It Safe! If your child is under age five, use Goldfish crackers or dry cereal, like Cheerios, instead of popcorn.

1. Pour popcorn into a bowl. Place the bowl on a table or hold it in your hands.

Thanks. We had great fun.
We couldn't stop giggling.
—John Donegan,
Atlanta, Georgia

2. Have your child place her hands behind her back.

3. Ask her to pick up the popcorn with no hands. Ask her to try picking it up using only her teeth, then using only her lips, and then using only her tongue. Show her how to do these tasks if she is not sure how to do them. How many pieces can she pick up at one time? Is it easier if she picks up the popcorn using her lips and teeth working together? What about when she also uses her tongue together with her lips and teeth? How can she pick up the popcorn with just her tongue? What makes the popcorn stick?

4. Have her try picking up other snack foods with no hands. Are some foods easier to pick up than others? Why?

Shoebox Sounds

What You Will Do

Place your child's toys in a shoebox one at a time and shake the box. Can he guess which toy is in the box by the sound it makes?

Your Child

If your child is under age five, use only two or three toys. If he has trouble guessing which toy it is, try playing with all of the toys first and listening to the sounds they make. Then, put one of the toys in the box and shake the box.

Fact

Children's toys make sounds that are recognizable. Just as we can recall items from memory by sight, so too can we recall items by the sounds they make.

What You Need

★ 5 toys
★ Towel or blanket
★ Shoebox with a lid

1. Collect several of your child's toys and place them on the floor. Let your child look at the toys for a few seconds and then cover them with the towel.

2. Reach under the towel and grab a toy. Place it in the shoebox, without your child seeing it, and put the lid on the box.

3. Shake the box. Ask your child to listen to the sound and guess which toy is in the box. Shake the box again slowly if he needs to hear it again.

4. Continue the guessing game until your child identifies all of the items. Give him some hints if he needs help.

An Extra Bite

Have your child play stump the parent. Select a large group of objects for the child to choose from (to avoid any valuable or breakable objects being damaged). See if he can find objects that you cannot guess by their sound.

 I enjoyed this so much I tried it at a party with my grown-up friends. It worked there too!
—*Kris Smothers, Annapolis, Maryland*

Toss It!

What You Will Do

Toss different kinds of balls into a paper bag. Some balls will be easier to toss into the bag than others.

Your Child

Your child may not have developed throwing skills yet. Help her if she needs it, so she will not get discouraged. You may also want to try making a larger target, such as an empty box, so your child will have an easier time hitting it and will feel successful.

Fact

The balls used in this activity are made from different materials. Some are lighter and some are heavier than others. The weight of an object affects the way it travels a specific distance. Heavy objects may not need to be tossed as hard to reach a target as lightweight objects.

What You Need

★ Paper bag or an empty box
★ Material to make different types of balls—aluminum foil, newspaper, paper towels, tissue, or clay

1. Place a paper bag about five feet away from your child.

2. Ask her to toss a small ball into the bag. If she needs to practice tossing the ball, allow her a few minutes to do so. She may need to stand a little closer or farther away from the bag.

3. Ask her to predict which of the balls will make it into the bag. Now, have her try tossing the other balls into the bag. What does she notice about the balls when she tosses them? Which ones are easier to toss into the bag? Does she have to change anything about the way she tosses the different balls?

4. Move the bag farther away. Which balls are easier for her to toss into the bag? Does she have to toss them differently to get them to reach the bag?

Walk This Way

What You Will Do

This activity demonstrates how animals move and how their bodies are built to move the way they do. The activity can be done either inside or outside. If done inside, use a hallway or room without breakable items.

44

Fact

Legs come in many shapes and sizes. Kangaroos and frogs have legs that are good for hopping and leaping, while ducks have legs that are good for walk-ing *and* swimming. During this activity, your child will imitate the way several animals walk. It's not going to be an exact imitation because our legs are not meant to do the same thing as a kanga-roo's legs. By imitating and observing many animals, your child will have an idea of how hopping legs and leaping legs are designed.

What You Need

- ★ Wrist watch with a second hand
- ★ Pencil
- ★ Plain white paper
- ★ Measuring tape
- ★ 2 books

 A little lass, looking at a rabbit, exclaimed: "Look, mama! The rabbit winked its nose at me."

1. Have your child select three animals whose walk he can imitate. He might waddle like a duck, leap like a frog, or hop like a kangaroo.

2. Write the three animals on the piece of paper in three separate columns. Ask your child which animal walk he thinks will be the fastest and draw a star next to it.

3. Ask him to place a book on the floor to indicate a starting line. Then measure 10 feet from the starting point to determine a finishing line and place the second book at that location.

4. Now ask your child to stand at the starting point, and when you say go, he will walk like one of the animals he selected. Time him until he reaches the finish line. Tell him the time it took him to reach the finish and help him record it on the paper in the appropriate column.

5. Let him catch his breath and then proceed with the other animals by repeating step 4.

6. After he has completed all three animals, look at the results together. Which animal walk was the fastest? Which one was the easiest? How did his prediction compare to the result?

7. Repeat the activity selecting three other animals.

An Extra Bite

Look at an animal book particularly observing the shape and size of the different animals' legs. Discuss what the animals use their legs for, and compare them with other animals' legs and what they are used for.

If you have several children, try this activity as a game. Write several animal names on slips of paper and put them in a hat. Ask each child to draw a piece of paper from the hat. Each child will demonstrate the animal he or she selects, and the other children will guess which animal is being imitated.

Try using a theme, for example, flying or slithering animals, animals at a zoo or in a forest, or insects and reptiles.

What Makes a Foot?

What You Will Do

Your child will measure items using her hands or feet as the measuring tool.

Your Child

If your child is younger than six, do steps 1 and 2 only. If your child appears interested, continue with step 3. Children in this age group may only be interested in steps 1 and 2 along with a short discussion about measuring. You could also talk about other types of measuring, such as measuring liquids.

Fact

There are standard measurement tools that people use to communicate correctly. If we go to the lumberyard and ask for a six-foot piece of wood and use our feet to measure it with, we may not get a long enough piece of wood. The person at the lumberyard uses a standard measurement of 12 inches to cut wood. We need to use the same standard if we want to get the correct size piece of wood. Imagine the confusion if everyone measured with a different measuring tool!

What You Need

★ Sofa
★ Tape measure

1. You and your child will use your feet first to take a measurement.

2. Put your foot against your child's foot. Ask her if she notices any differences or similarities between her foot and your foot.

3. Predict how many feet long the sofa is using her feet as the measurement tool. Ask her to measure the sofa with her feet by walking along the side of the sofa heel to toe. You may need to show her how to walk heel to toe.

4. Compare the prediction to the result. Now ask her to predict how many of your feet long the sofa is. If she has trouble with this, remind her of the differences and similarities between your feet. Compare the result with your child's prediction.

5. Now, measure the sofa with the tape measure. What measurement do you get in standard feet? Is the measurement the same as when you measured with your feet?

6. Repeat the activity measuring another object or using another measurement tool, such as your hands.

3

Quiet Times

• •

Looking for ways to calm the savage beast or
just a quiet activity for a lazy afternoon? Here are
some wholesome nibbles that fill the bill.

Can You Hear It?

What You Will Do

With paper-towel and toilet-paper tubes, your child will listen to the sounds in your house. You will need to collect the tubes in advance.

Fact

Our ears are able to hear many sounds because the outer ear helps to collect them. When we hold a tube up to our ear, sounds are amplified because we are extending our outer ear.

Play It Safe! Do not allow your child to walk or run with the tube up to his ear or eye.

What You Need

- ★ Paper-towel tube
- ★ Toilet-paper tube

1. Walk around the house with your child and listen for sounds. Some will be soft sounds while others will be loud.

2. Ask him if he thinks the sounds will be louder or softer when he listens to them through the cardboard tubes.

3. Give your child the tubes. Have him listen to the sounds through the toilet-paper tube. Do these sounds sound different than without the tube? Are the sounds louder? Can he hear new sounds?

4. Now have him listen with the paper-towel tube. What does he notice about the sounds? Are they louder or softer? Is the sound louder through the long or the short tube?

Hidden Message

What You Will Do

Your child will hide a message to you in a picture.

Your Child

If your child is just learning to read and write, keep it simple! Help her write her name or letters of the alphabet.

Fact

Animals use camouflage both to hide themselves in their environment so enemies cannot see them and to sneak up on their prey. We can hide messages in the same way by making the words blend in with a picture or the colors we use around the message.

What You Need

★ Plain white paper
★ Crayons or markers

1. Ask your child to think of a short message she wants to send to someone.

2. Have her write the message on the paper.

3. Have her draw a picture or color the paper to camouflage the message.

4. Ask her to deliver the hidden message. Can the message be detected?

An Extra Bite

Try to camouflage other things. From a piece of white paper, cut out circles in several different sizes. Choose a room in the house and color the circles the same colors that are in the room in order to "hide" them. Ask your child to find all of the circles.

A teacher wrote on the back of a student's essay, "Please write more legibly." The next day the student went up to her and asked, "What is this you've written? I can't make it out."

How Much Can You See?

What You Will Do

This activity uses visual images and memory to identify objects.

Fact

Our eyes and brain work together to help us remember things that we have seen before. Even if only a portion of an item is seen, sometimes it is just enough to spark a memory. If the item is familiar, we remember it more quickly than an unfamiliar one.

What You Need

★ Circle patterns on the next page
★ 3 sheets of plain white paper
★ Pencil or pen
★ Scissors (Use safety scissors if the child will be cutting.)
★ Books and toys small enough to be hidden by a sheet of paper

1. Using the circles on the following page, help your child trace one circle in the middle of each sheet of paper and cut it out. There should be one circle per sheet.

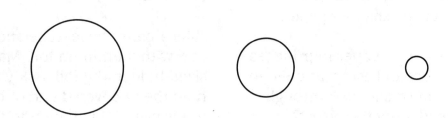

2. Ask your child to close his eyes. Place a book or toy on the floor in front of him. Lay the sheet of paper with the smallest hole on top of the object. No peeking under the sheet of paper!

3. Hold the sheet of paper four inches above the object and ask your child to kneel on the floor and look through the hole. Can he identify the object?

4. Now cover the object with the sheet of paper with the medium-sized hole. Can he identify the object now? Use the third sheet of paper with the largest hole if needed.

5. Choose another object and repeat steps 2–4.

An Extra Bite

Take a paper-towel tube and cover one end with aluminum foil. Make a pencil-sized hole in the foil. Ask your child to hold the uncovered end of the tube up to his eye. Hold an item in front of him. (Do not allow him to walk or run with the tube up to his eye.) Can he identify the object? Ask him to move the tube up and down, and side to side, so he can see more of the object. Save the tube and use it like a viewfinder to locate toys that need to be put away.

Magnify It

What You Will Do

Make a magnifying glass from a clear plastic bag and water.

Fact

The water in this activity acts much like a magnifying glass. Light bends and spreads out as it passes through the water in the same way as it does through a magnifying glass. This action causes the image being viewed to appear larger or magnified. Even though we cannot actually see the light bending and spreading, we can see the result. The amount of water the light must pass through affects the degree to which magnification occurs. If more water is added, the magnification will increase. The magnification decreases if the water is reduced.

What You Need

- ★ Zip-top plastic bag made for freezing
- ★ Water
- ★ Masking tape or duct tape
- ★ Book or newspaper

1. Ask your child to help you fill the plastic bag with water. The bag should be completely full but still able to be sealed properly.

2. Seal the bag and cover the seal with tape for extra security.

3. Ask your child to select a book or newspaper. Ask her what she thinks will happen to the words when the bag is placed on the page.

4. Place the bag on the page and ask her what she notices about the letters and words when she looks through the bag. Have her look through the bag from different angles.

5. Carefully lift the bag off the page while she is still looking at it. Move the bag farther away from the book then close up again. What happens to the letters and words as you do this?

6. Ask her to carefully place the bag on other items around the house. What does she notice about the items when she views them through the bag?

An Extra Bite

Fill several plastic bags with different amounts of water. Let your child discover the relationship between the amount of water and the amount of magnification.

Mirror Images

What You Will Do

You and your child will try to do several tasks while looking in a mirror.

Fact

A mirror reverses an image, and when you look into the mirror, your eyes send a message to your brain that is opposite of what it knows. Simple tasks that we do every day, such as buttoning a shirt or squeezing toothpaste on our toothbrush, become a little confusing for our brain when we use a mirror, causing your brain to say, "Slow down! I am not sure what you are asking me to do." We really have to think about what we are doing when we use a mirror to complete a task.

What You Need

★ Mirror
★ Shirt with buttons or snaps
★ Toothpaste
★ Toothbrush
★ Piece of plain white paper
★ Crayon or marker

61

1. Ask your child to stand in front of the mirror and button his shirt looking only in the mirror. Does he have any trouble? What does he notice about buttoning the shirt? Is it difficult to button the shirt while looking in the mirror?

2. Now, have him look in the mirror and try squeezing toothpaste onto his toothbrush. Does he have to go slowly and really think about which way to move?

3. Have him write his name on a piece of paper. Ask him what he thinks will happen when he holds the piece of paper in front of the mirror. Have him hold the paper up with the writing facing the mirror. What does he notice about his name? Can he read it? Can he rewrite his name so he can read it in the mirror?

An Extra Bite

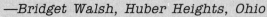

Try the next activity, Mirror Me, to learn how a mirror reverses images.

> [My] daughter thought she'd have no trouble doing things in the mirror image, but realized there was more to it than meets the eye.
> —Bridget Walsh, Huber Heights, Ohio

Mirror Me

What You Will Do

You and your child will sit face to face and mirror each other. This is a fun way to show a child that a mirror reverses images.

Your Child

Children like to mimic others, especially you! Mirror Me helps funnel this interest into a fun and productive activity.

Fact

Mirrors can be deceiving and difficult to figure out. We know mirrors reflect our image, however, it is a reversed image.

This may make it difficult to stand in front of a mirror and complete even the simplest, most routine tasks. For example, our hands and brain know how to button a shirt, but try it while looking in a mirror. When we look in the mirror, our eyes are sending a different message to our brain about what the hands have to do to button the shirt. So the brain gets a little confused and must slow down to compensate for the reversed image projected from the mirror.

What You Need

★ Mirror
★ Partner

1. Have your child stand in front of a mirror and make movements, such as nodding or shaking her head.

2. Now, ask her to sit or stand in front of you. Explain that you want her to pretend she is a mirror and copy the movement you make.

3. Start with easy movements like waving or pointing to your knee. What does your child notice about being a mirror? Do both of you move the same arm? If you move your right arm, which arm is your child moving?

4. Now, ask her to stand behind you and copy your movements. What is different about her movements? Are both of you moving the same arm?

5. Try mirroring again. This time you copy your child's movements.

An Extra Bite

For more fun with reversed images try the previous activity, Mirror Images.

Shoe Show

What You Will Do

Children like to try on and walk in other people's shoes. In this activity, you will be shoe detectives, helping your child make observations about different shoes.

Your Child

If your child is under age five, start by looking at the shoes and asking him to describe the shoes by color and size (big and small). This will help him understand how to observe the shoes. Older children will be able to guess the type (dress or casual) or purpose of the shoes (work or play).

Fact

Science uses and requires skills such as observation, pattern recognition, and classification. This activity introduces your child to these various techniques. We observe objects to determine similarities and differences or patterns, and based on our observations, we classify the object. For example, plants and animals are classified into species and families based on specific characteristics that are observed in them.

What You Need

★ Several pairs of shoes (Include a few pairs of your shoes and your child's shoes. Make sure they are different in appearance and purpose.)

1. Have your child select two different shoes and put them on. Ask him how the shoes feel on his feet. Is it hard for him to walk with the shoes he selected?

2. Ask him to select a pair of your shoes. Observe this pair and a pair of your child's shoes. How are they different? How are they similar?

3. Have him put your shoes on and try to walk. How do the shoes fit? Is it easy to walk in them?

4. Selecting from the remaining shoes, have him predict which shoes will be the easiest and hardest for him to walk in.

5. Have him group similar shoes together, such as shoes with laces, slip-on shoes, dress shoes, and play shoes. Do any of the shoes fit into several groups?

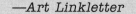

The next time you talk to a little child, look deeply into his eyes. Don't just glance at him, or over him, or through him. Look straight through those wide-open, unguarded eye portals into his mind. You'll feel an answering, almost forgotten stirring in your mind. You'll be in touch with innocence and the long ago. Do it—for it's one of the best things in life.
—*Art Linkletter*

Tea Time

What You Will Do

By adding sugar and milk to hot and iced tea, you and your child will see what happens to liquids and solids in hot and cold water.

Fact

Temperature is the speed at which molecules move. The molecules in hot water move faster than molecules in cold water. The fast-moving molecules in hot water hit the sugar and break its bonds, causing the sugar to dissolve. It takes longer to dissolve sugar in cold water because the water molecules are not moving as fast. Sometimes we stir iced tea to help dissolve the sugar that has fallen to the bottom of the glass. Stirring exposes the sugar once again to the moving molecules causing the sugar bonds to break and dissolve. If there is too much sugar, the water becomes saturated and cannot dissolve any more sugar. The excess sugar will fall to the bottom of the glass.

Play It Safe! Pour the hot water for your child and be sure she does not touch the glass. Wash your hands before doing this activity.

What You Need

* ★ 2 tall clear glasses that will each hold 1½ cups of water
* ★ 2 tea bags
* ★ Measuring cups
* ★ 1½ cups of cold water
* ★ 1½ cups of hot water
* ★ 3 ice cubes
* ★ Measuring teaspoon
* ★ 2 teaspoons sugar
* ★ 2 teaspoons milk

1. Have your child pour the cold water into one glass. Then ask her to add one tea bag and three ice cubes. Watch what happens to the tea bag.

2. Carefully pour the hot water into the other glass and ask your child to place the other tea bag in the glass. Watch what happens to the tea bag.

3. Place the glass with the cold water next to the glass with the hot water. Ask your child to guess which glass of water, the hot or cold, will dissolve the sugar more quickly once it is added.

4. Add one teaspoon of sugar to each glass. What happens to the sugar? Where does it go? Does it dissolve faster in one of the glasses than in the other? Will stirring help dissolve the sugar? Which one needs to be stirred?

5. Now, add one teaspoon of milk to each glass. What happens to the milk? Does it react the same way the sugar did? Are there any differences in the way the milk reacted in the cold water and in the hot water?

 Dream lofty dreams and as you dream, so shall you become; your vision is the promise of what you shall one day be.
—*James Allen, American novelist*

Tooth Talk

Ages 5 and Up

What You Will Do

You will make impressions of your child's teeth in cookie dough and then compare the impressions. Identify which teeth do the cutting and which do the chewing.

Fact

Children have different sized and shaped teeth than adults. Children's teeth are smaller and shaped differently because of the size of their jaws and the types of foods they eat. As children get older, their baby teeth are replaced by permanent teeth. The permanent teeth are larger to accommodate growing children and the types of foods they eat.

What You Need

★ Cookie dough (premade or made from your favorite recipe)
★ Cookie sheet (if you plan to bake the impressions)

Tips Allow additional time if you are making your own dough. The dough works best if it is slightly frozen (about 30 minutes in the freezer).

Play It Safe! Some children have a gag reflex. If your child has a gag reflex, use care in making the impressions by not placing the dough too far back in his mouth. Also, your child will probably want to eat the cookie dough. Most cookie dough contains raw eggs, so this is probably not a good idea because of the possibility of salmonella.

71

1. Ask your child to tear off a piece of dough large enough to fit in the palm of his hand.

2. Ask him to roll the dough on the counter until it is between four to six inches long. Make sure the dough is not too thin or too long to fit in his mouth.

3. Now, ask him to open his mouth and carefully lay the dough on his lower teeth. If there is too much dough, tear some off; if there is not enough dough, add some to the roll. Ask your child to close his mouth and softly bite into the dough.

4. Have him open his mouth and help him remove the dough.

5. Make your teeth impressions in another piece of dough and compare them with your child's impressions. What differences and similarities are there between the two impressions? Can you tell which teeth do which jobs? Which teeth cut food and which ones do the chewing?

6. Bake your impressions just as you would normally bake the cookies. Once they're baked, eat them, but be sure to eat your own impressions!

An Extra Bite

Try to make impressions in other types of foods. How about with a slice of bread or in an apple?

Make a mold of your child's teeth by pouring wax from a candle into the cookie dough impression. Follow steps 1 through 4 above and then light a candle and carefully tip the candle as it burns so the wax pours into the impressions.

What Color Is It?

What You Will Do

Select several different colored sheets of construction paper and have your child try to guess the color of the sheets in the dark.

Your Child

If your child is under age five, be sure to select colors she knows. Use only one or two sheets of construction paper and show her the colors before going into a dark room.

Fact

The retinas of our eyes contain two types of photoreceptors—cones and rods. Cones are responsible for color vision, but they only work when there is light. By contrast, rods can capture light even when it is quite dark. Rods, however, do not distinguish colors, only black and white. At night or in the dark, only our rods are at work.

What You Need

★ 5 different colors of construction paper (both dark and light colors)
★ Piece of plain white paper
★ Pencil or pen
★ Dark room

1. Number the sheets of colored paper and place them in order. Do not show your child the colored sheets. On the sheet of white paper number from one to five. You will record your child's guesses on this sheet of paper.

2. Go into a dark room, bringing the colored paper and the numbered sheet with you. Ask your child to tell you when her eyes have "adjusted" to the darkness.

3. When she is ready, hold the first colored sheet in front of her and ask her to identify the color of the paper. Record her guess on your sheet of paper—as best you can in the dark!

4. When she has guessed a color for each sheet, turn the light on and compare her guesses with the actual colors. How many did she guess correctly?

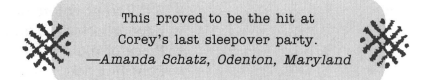

This proved to be the hit at Corey's last sleepover party.
—Amanda Schatz, Odenton, Maryland

Without a Sound

What You Will Do

Communicate messages or show emotions using only nonverbal cues.

Your Child

Use simple emotions if your child is under age five, and spend a few more minutes on step 1. Steps 1 and 2 are most appropriate for a younger child.

Fact

People often speak without saying a word. Messages or emotions can be conveyed with a simple gesture or movement, and no words need to be spoken. While there are certain nonverbal cues that are common to everyone, other cues may not be as easy to interpret.

Sometimes a gesture, expression, or motion may mean one thing to one person and something totally different to another person.

An easy definition for *nonverbal* is giving a message without talking.

What You Need

★ Magazine or book
★ Mirror (optional)

1. Look through a magazine or book with your child and ask him to point out people who look happy, sad, surprised, or mad. Ask him how he knows the person's feelings.

2. Now, try telling him that you are happy using only nonverbal cues. Then

ask him to try giving you a nonverbal message about how he feels.

3. Ask him to try relating a little more elaborate message, such as he is hungry or it is time to go to bed.

4. On the count of three, both of you make a face that shows surprise. Are your expressions the same? Look at your expressions in a mirror. Are there some differences in your expressions even though you both were trying to express the same emotion?

An Extra Bite

Make emotion masks out of paper plates and Popsicle sticks. Then, act out a simple play together wearing your masks.

 Of all the things you wear, your expression is the most important. —*Unknown*

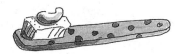

4

Bedtime

• • • • • • • • • •

Turn bedtime into science time.
These fun activities will enrich even
the most mundane bedtime routines.

One, Two, Pick Up My Room

What You Will Do

Need a little help cleaning up? Ask your child to put her toys away using only her fingers and toes.

Fact

Our hands and feet allow us to do many things. Together our hands can clap, drive a car, or type. When our feet work together, we can walk, run, or ride a bicycle. Our hands and feet have parts —fingers and toes—that work together to accomplish tasks for us. When we ask our fingers and toes to work individually, it may seem very uncomfortable because we do not normally use our fingers and toes this way. What happens when we want a finger and toe to work together? Now that's confusing! But, it can be done. We just have to go slowly and think more about how our fingers and toes are moving.

What You Need

. . . .

★ **Messy room**

1. Ask your child to look at her hands and feet and to move her fingers and toes together and individually.

2. Now, challenge her to put away her toys using only her fingers and toes. Have her try picking up toys with her two pinky fingers or with an index finger and her big toe.

3. Ask her to think of other finger and toe combinations and try them. Try some of these with her. You will have a good laugh.

 An ounce of example is worth a pound of advice.

Making Waves

What You Will Do

This a great bath-time activity that asks your child to predict how high a wave he can make in the tub using his hands and other wave makers. This activity can also be done in a swimming pool.

Fact

Making waves in the bathtub can be a lot of fun. Just how are waves made? When you place your hand in the water and move it, you are pushing water out of the way of your hand and creating motion in the water. This motion creates small waves. Moving your hand faster results in stronger motion and larger waves.

What You Need

- ★ Bathtub
- ★ Wave makers, such as a spatula or large spoon

1. Prepare your child's bath.

Tip You probably do not want to fill the tub too full.

2. Ask him to get in the tub. Tell him that you want to see how big a wave he can make in the tub.

3. Sit at the opposite end of the tub— you do not have to be in the tub! Hold your hand two inches above the water.

4. Ask your child to make a wave with his hand. Did it touch your hand? Did the wave go over your hand?

5. Take turns with your child. Have him hold his hand at the point you think

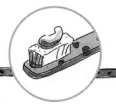

your wave will reach. Did your wave touch his hand? What is the difference between your waves and his waves? Do bigger hands make bigger waves?

6. Repeat these steps, and use the wave makers this time. Do the wave makers create higher waves than your hands or your child's?

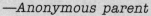

"Are we in trouble for putting all this water on the floor?" Making Waves can be messy fun. Children are taught not to splash too much while they are in the bathtub. Sometimes it is OK to let the children really get involved even if it makes a mess. What's a little water, right?
—*Anonymous parent*

Shower Sounds

What You Will Do

Your child will let the water from the shower hit different parts of her body. She will listen to the way the water sounds when she has her ears plugged. This activity could also be done outside with a hose sprayer in the summertime. You will want to try this yourself before asking your child to do the activity. This way you will know what it sounds like when the water hits different parts of the body.

Fact

We can hear sounds from inside our body when we plug our ears. When water hits different parts of the body, the sound we hear is the vibration off of different body tissues. Our back is more boney than our stomach, so the sound will be louder where there are more bones. Soft tissue like our stomach will create softer vibrations. The loudness of the sound also depends on how far away the body part is from your ears.

What You Need

. . . .

★ **Shower**

1. Move the showerhead down as low as possible to your child.

2. Ask your child to get in the shower and let the water hit different parts of her body, such as her head, back, chest, stomach, and legs. Then, ask her to plug her ears and listen to the water hitting her body again.

3. Ask her to describe to you the variance in the sound when the water hits different parts of her body. Why are the sounds different? Does it matter how far away from her ears the water is hitting? What other action affects the sound? Does cupping her ears with her hands change what she hears?

 Anything that helps get Joshua into the bath or shower is great. Thanks.
—*George Mossouri,*
Annapolis, Maryland

Water Levels

What You Will Do

Your child will stand, sit, and lie in a bathtub partially filled with water and look at the change in water level each time he changes position.

Fact

Water levels in a bathtub rise when items are added to the water. When your child stands in the tub you may notice the water rise slightly, and when he sits in the tub the water will rise a little more. The water level rises more when he sits because there is more of him in the water than just his feet. This is similar to when you add ice to a glass of soda. The more ice you add, the higher the soda level rises in the glass.

What You Need

★ Bathtub
★ 4 different colored bathtub crayons

1. Prepare your child's bath. Ask him where he thinks the water level will be when he stands in the tub. Have him use a bathtub crayon to mark this. Ask him where he thinks the water level will be when he sits and then when he lies in the tub. Have him mark these places too, with the same crayon.

2. Before he gets into the bathtub, mark the water level with the other colored bathtub crayon.

3. Help him step into the tub and stand. Have him look to see if he notices any change in the water level. If there is a change, mark where the top of the water is with the different colored crayon.

4. Now, have him sit in the tub. After the water stops moving, ask him what he notices about the water level. Mark the new level with the different colored crayon. Repeat step 4 if another child is going to get in the tub. What happens to the water level with two children in the tub?

5. If possible, have him lie down in the tub while supporting his head. If the water level rises, mark the new level with a different colored crayon.

6. Show your child all of the marks indicating the new water levels. Is more of his body in the water when the water level rises? What are other ways to raise the water level?

What's on the Wall?

What You Will Do

This is a bedtime activity that helps a child understand how her eyes work in light and dark and what she may see during the transition. This activity may help a child who is afraid of what she sees in her room when the lights go out.

Your Child

Many young children are afraid of the dark. You can help your child with her fears by trying this activity using a flashlight. Give her a flashlight and turn it on. Before you turn the room light off, ask her what she sees. Then turn the light off. Make sure she knows you will turn it back on if she gets scared. This way she will feel more in control of her situation. When the flashlight is off, ask her

what she sees. If she does not see every-thing she saw before the flashlight was turned off, ask her if she thinks any-thing has changed. Now, turn the flash-light back on and ask her what she sees.

Fact

Our eyes need time to refocus when we move from a light environment to a dark one. During the refocusing, we may not be able to see objects, even if we know they are there. As things begin to take shape, our eyes may be seeing incomplete objects; our brain is trying to determine what the object is but may not be able to recall the item.

What You Need

★ Room with a light and a door

1. With the light on, tuck your child in bed and together look around the room at the different items.

2. Shut the door and turn the light off. Ask her what she sees. Wait about 30 sec-onds. What does she see now? Does she recognize any of the things in her room? Do any of them look different to her with the light off? Does she see things that she did not see with the light on?

3. Turn the light back on. Is everything in the room the same? Try this a couple of times to help your child feel more comfortable in the dark.

As hoped for, this activity helped dispel some of our son's fears about going to bed at night.
—*Lynn Dorker, Edgewater, Maryland*

5

Bigger than a Bite

• •

Got some time? Try these mind-stretching activities
on weekends, rainy days, or school breaks.

Hot Sweaty Trees

What You Will Do

By placing a plastic bag around the leaves of a tree, you will make the tree sweat. This activity works best outside on a warm summer day; however, it can also be done inside with a tropical plant that sits in a warm sunny place.

Fact

. . . .

The leaves of plants and trees have pores, which are tiny holes. The pores can expand or contract depending on the temperature. In a warm environment, like the one you will create with the plastic bag and the sun, the pores open and release moisture. This is similar to how our bodies sweat when our temperature rises. In this activity the moisture enters the air inside the bag and collects on the sides where we can see it.

What You Need

. . . .

* ★ Large, clear resealable bag and 2 feet of string (if bag without a seal is used)
* ★ Branch of a live, leafy tree in a sunny place
* ★ Measuring cup

As a scientist, it's wonderful to find someone developing activities for young children that involve making predictions and collecting data.
—*Janice Seeworth, Arnold, Maryland*

1. Help your child find a tree branch with many healthy leaves. The tree needs to be in a warm sunny place.

2. Ask him to place the plastic bag around the tree branch. Caution him to be careful not to break or damage the tree in any way while placing the branch in the bag.

3. Close the open end of the bag by sealing it or tying it securely with a piece of string.

4. Ask your child to predict what will be in the bag in an hour.

5. Come back in one hour and carefully remove the bag from the branch. Take a look. What do you see?

6. Pour the water that has collected into a measuring cup. *Do not drink the water.* How much water collected? How do the leaves look compared to other leaves on the tree? Look at the leaves again the next day. Do they look any different?

Let the Sun Shine In

What You Will Do

You will need a sunny day for this activity. Your child will investigate where in the house the sun shines in at a certain time of the day. She will check the house again at a different time of the day to see in which rooms the sun is still shining.

Fact

As the earth rotates, the sun's light shines in different parts of our homes. The sun will shine in different parts of your house at different times of the day depending on the direction your house faces in relation to the sun. The season of the year may also determine where the sun shines in your house, and it may differ considerably from summer to winter.

What You Need

- ★ Circle pattern on the next page
- ★ Sheet of white paper
- ★ Pencil
- ★ Several sheets of yellow construction paper
- ★ Scissors (Use safety scissors if your child will be doing the cutting.)
- ★ Tape
- ★ Watch or clock

1. Trace the circle pattern on the following page by placing the white sheet of paper on top of it and drawing the pattern on the paper. Cut out this circle. Place this circle on top of the yellow construction paper and trace around it. Make two yellow circles for every room in your home. Cut these out. (Note: there may be extra circles when the activity is complete.)

2. In the morning, ask your child to go to each room in your house. Is the sun shining in the room? If it is, ask her to tape a yellow circle on the door to the room. Write the time on the yellow circle.

3. In the afternoon, have her tape the remaining circles to the doors of rooms in which the sun is shining. How many rooms have two yellow circles? What does your child notice about the rooms that have two yellow circles and the ones that have only one yellow circle?

Why does the sun shine in some rooms all day, while in other rooms it shines only in the morning or afternoon, but not both?

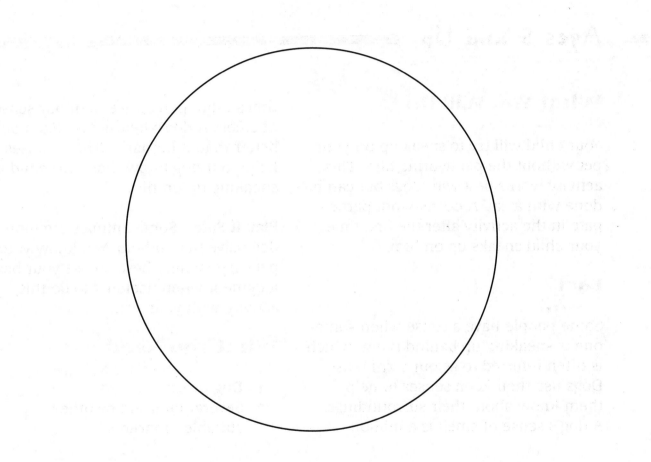

Pet Play

What You Will Do

Your child will try to sneak up on your pet without the pet hearing him. This activity works best with dogs but can be done with a cat. A cat may not participate in the activity after the first time your child sneaks up on him.

Fact

Some people have a sense when someone is sneaking up behind them, which is often referred to as our *sixth sense*. Dogs use their keen senses to help them know about their surroundings. A dog's sense of smell is a million times more perceptive than our sense of smell. A dog's hearing is also much better than a human's. These senses help your dog know that your child is sneaking up on him.

Play It Safe! Some animals are more defensive than others. You know your pet's personality best, so use your best judgment when deciding to do this activity with your pet.

What You Need

★ Dog or cat
★ Several quarters or other suitable "markers"

1. Ask your child to quietly find your dog or cat in the house. When he finds your pet, have him place a quarter on the floor where he is standing. You will need to help your child remember approximately where the pet is standing or sitting.

2. Wait a few minutes and then have your child slowly and quietly walk up to your pet, trying to get as close as possible without the pet hearing him.

3. When your pet hears your child, have your child stop and place another quarter on the floor at that spot. You will place a quarter where the pet is (or was) sitting. Count the number of steps from the first quarter to the quarter where the pet is (or was) sitting to determine how far away your child was when he started sneaking up on your pet. How close did your child get to the pet?

4. Ask your child to count the number of steps from the quarter marking where the pet heard him to the quarter where the pet is (or was) sitting.

5. What did the pet do when he heard your child? Did he run away? Did he just look at him? Did he act scared?

6. Now, try to get the pet to sit. Have your child slowly walk up to him. How close can he get this time? Ask your child to try it again but to move quickly or make a noise this time. Ask your child to describe how your pet reacts this time. Does the pet react differently to your child's actions?

A harried father was listening to his seven-year-old son scratch away on his violin, while the family dog howled an accompaniment. After a few minutes of the dissonant practice session, the father asked the son, "Can't you play something the dog doesn't know?"

Pint-Sized Playground

What You Will Do

Children like to build things. This activity uses your child's building skills on a small scale to create a miniature playground.

Fact

Architects and building engineers use their design and imaginative skills to develop ideas for structures; they often build a scale model of the structure to determine if the design is safe or pleasing. In this activity your child will use memory to help her recall what playground equipment looks like, and scale to help her build the equipment to the desired size.

What You Need

★ Sticks
★ Leaves
★ Rocks

1. Locate an area outside to build the miniature playground.

2. Explain to your child that she is going to build a playground small enough for ladybugs. Discuss with her what she wants in the playground, such as a swing or a slide.

3. Have her collect sticks, twigs, leaves, and rocks with which to build the playground.

4. Start building! Help your child identify how the building items can be used to make playground equipment.

5. Challenge her to build a new piece of playground equipment, such as a teeter-totter.

An Extra Bite

Use Legos, Lincoln Logs, or similar construction toys to build an indoor pint-sized playground.

Vanishing Colors

What You Will Do

Things that are white in color are really made up of many colors, and things that are many colors can be made to look white. This activity demonstrates this phenomenon using a bicycle wheel; it may take a half an hour or more.

Fact

Our eyes can see images of all shapes and sizes. They do, however, have limitations on how fast an image can be focused on the retina (back of the eye) and recognized. Our eyes need at least $\frac{1}{18}$ of a second to refocus and recognize when we look from one object to another. When a bicycle wheel begins to turn, we can see the individual colors on the spokes, but as the wheel turns faster and faster, the colors are moving at a speed that exceeds the rate at which our eyes can keep up. So, we see gray or white instead of the red, blue, and yellow colors.

What You Need

★ Plain white paper
★ Pencil
★ Scissors
★ 2 pieces of each color construction paper—red, blue, and yellow
★ Pattern provided on the next page
★ Masking tape or duct tape
★ Bicycle
★ Brightly lit area

Play It Safe! Make sure your child keeps his fingers out of the spokes of the turning bicycle wheel.

1. Ask your child to place the white paper over the pattern provided on the next page. Trace the pattern and cut it out.

2. Now, draw the pattern twice on each of the sheets of construction paper and cut the patterns out. When your child is done, he should have four patterns of each color.

3. Find a brightly lit area outside and help your child turn the bicycle upside down so the wheels are pointing in the air. Help him tape the pieces of colored paper to the spokes of the back wheel, alternating each color around the center of the wheel—red, blue, yellow, red, blue, yellow. Do not fold or bend the taped paper. (You may have a few pieces of paper left over.)

4. Fasten each piece of paper securely with tape. Ask your child what he thinks will happen to the colors when the wheel spins. Turn the pedals so the back wheel starts to spin and continue turning the pedals so the wheel spins swiftly. *Keep all body parts away from the spinning wheel.*

5. Ask your child to stand about six feet away and look at the wheel as it spins. What does he notice about the color of the paper in the wheel as it spins fast? What happens when the wheel starts to slow down? What makes the colors appear and disappear?

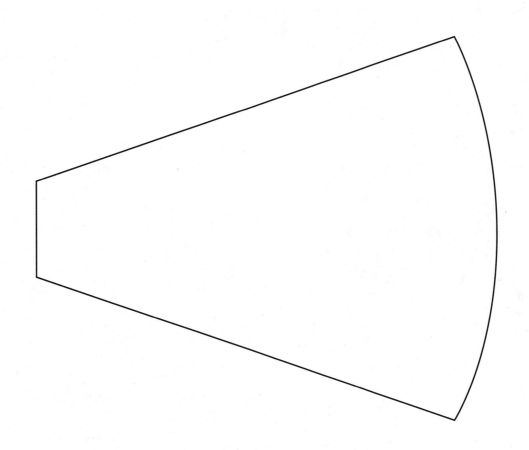

Bibliography

Barlett, John. *Bartlett's Familiar Quotations.*
14th ed. Boston, MA: Little, Brown and
Co., 1968.

Esar, Evan. *The Comic Encyclopedia.* New
York: Doubleday & Co., Inc., 1978.

Linkletter, Art. *The New Kids Say the
Darndest Things.* Ottawa, IL: Jameson
Books, Inc., 1995.

National Research Council. *National Science
Education Standards.* Washington, D.C.:
National Academy Press, 1996.

Prochnow, Herbert V. *A Speaker's Treasury.*
Grand Rapids, MI: Baker Book House
Company, 1973.

Young, Mark, ed. *Guinness Book of World
Records.* New York: Bantam Books,
1998.

Acknowledgments

We want to thank all of the people who had their hands and minds on this project and supported us through the various stages of *Bite-Sized Science*.

Many parents, homeschoolers, and child-care providers enthusiastically tested and gave us feedback about the activities in this book. Their input allowed us to select the most appropriate activities and make modifications to create what you see here. Thanks to all of our activity testers including Mary Ahearn, Arnold, Maryland; Lupito Alverez, Austin, Texas; Jennifer Anderson, Marysville, Ohio; Debbie O'Banion from the YWCA of Annapolis and Anne Arundel County, Maryland; Sandy Berry, Pasadena, Maryland; Lisa Nottingham-Blongé, Toronto, Canada; Carla Dawn Bynum, Pearl, Mississippi; Donna DeLawder; John Donegan, Atlanta, Georgia; Lynn Dorker, Edgewater, Maryland; Stephanie Duncan; Caryn Walaski, Dolphy Glendinning, Norman Randall, Vanessa Speaks, and Kerry Sullivan from the Annapolis Recreation and Parks, Maryland; Cynthia Hart, Pasadena, Maryland; Emil and Marie Keller; Penny Manchee, Toronto, Canada; Sarah McCormick, Annapolis, Maryland; Lisa Wiseman; George Mossouri, Annapolis, Maryland; Rebecca Musliner, Crofton, Maryland; Mildred Pertz, Akron, Ohio; Amanda Schatz, Odenton, Maryland; Janice Seeworth, Arnold, Maryland; Barbara Silver, Arnold, Maryland; Jay Smith; Kris Smothers, Annapolis, Maryland; Kelly Sullivan; Kelly Thomas, Edgewater, Maryland; and Bridget Walsh, Huber Heights, Ohio.

Thank you to David Anderson, Brisbane, Australia; Lisa Kensler, Annapolis, Maryland; Lynn Dierking, Annapolis, Maryland; Jodi Gronborg, Chicago, Illinois; and Robert Pruitt, Arnold, Maryland, for sharing their ideas and allowing us to develop them into activities. Their creativity and interest in providing fun learning experiences for children are reflected throughout this collection of activities.

A special thanks to Barbara Butler of the National Science Foundation.

Without her support and encouragement this book would not be possible.

A very special thanks from Kristi to Robert Pruitt, Institute for Learning Innovation, for his encouragement and advice throughout the idea generation and development of the activities. Thanks also to Jessica Luke, Institute for Learning Innovation, for managing the activity testing and for recruiting enthusiastic testers. We could not have done it without you, Luke!

About the Authors

John H. Falk is the founder, president, and director of the Institute for Learning Innovation. John has developed numerous science and educational materials. He was one of the coauthors, along with Kristi S. Rosenberg, of *Bubble Monster and Other Science Fun* also published by Chicago Review Press. John lives in Annapolis, Maryland, with his wife, Lynn, and has three children—Joshua, Dan, and Laura.

Kristi S. Rosenberg is a former associate at the Institute for Learning Innovation. Kristi's work focuses on providing informal educational opportunities in everyday experiences. Kristi lives in Edgewater, Maryland, with her very supportive husband and one-year-old son, Bryce.

More Activity Books for Young Children from Chicago Review Press

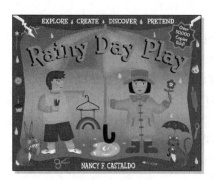

Rainy Day Play
Explore, Create, Discover, Pretend
Nancy F. Castaldo
"Any adult faced with a bored child or, worse yet, a whole roomful of them, will find this book a lifesaver."
—*School Library Journal*
ages 3–7
ISBN-13: 978-1-55652-563-6
ISBN-10: 1-55652-563-X
144 pages, paper, $12.95

Insectigations
40 Hands-on Activities to Explore the Insect World
Cindy Blobaum
From butterflies and beetles to crickets and katydids, these experiments, art projects, and games will bring out the entomologist in every kid.
ages 7–10
ISBN-13: 978-1-55652-568-1
ISBN-10: 1-55652-568-0
144 pages, paper, $12.95

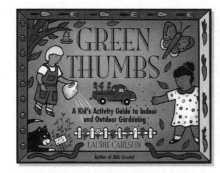

Play with Us

100 Games from Around the World
Oriol Ripoll
"Entertaining games and activities that are easy to learn."   —*Columbus Parent*
ages 5 & up
ISBN-13: 978-1-55652-594-0
ISBN-10: 1-55652-594-X
128 pages, paper, $16.95

Green Thumbs

A Kid's Activity Guide to Indoor and Outdoor Gardening
Laurie Carlson
Teach budding gardeners what it takes to make things grow with fun activities that require only readily available materials.
ages 5–12
ISBN-13: 978-1-55652-238-3
ISBN-10: 1-55652-238-X
144 pages, paper, $12.95

Sunny Days and Starry Nights
Nature Activities for Ages 2-6
Nancy F. Castaldo
"Points budding scientists down the
  right path."   —*School Library Journal*
ISBN-13: 978-1-55652-556-8
ISBN-10: 1-55652-556-7
144 pages, paper, $12.95

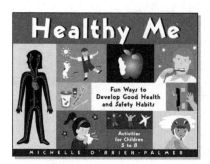

Healthy Me
*Fun Ways to Develop Good Health
and Safety Habits*
Michelle O'Brien-Palmer
Fun activities to introduce young children to basic health issues such as
germs, dental hygiene, nutrition, exercise, and safety.
ages 4–8
ISBN-13: 978-1-55652-359-5
ISBN-10: 1-55652-359-9
128 pages, paper, $12.95

Winter Day Play!
Activities, Crafts, and Games for Indoors and Out
Nancy F. Castaldo

"Chicago Review Press' series of activity books is top-rate and imaginative . . . This one's a definite must for snow-bound families and teachers."
—*Kids' Home Library*

ISBN-13: 978-1-55652-381-6
ISBN-10: 1-55652-381-5
176 pages, paper, $13.95

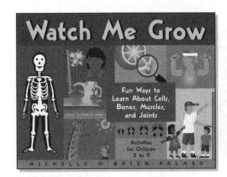

Watch Me Grow
Fun Ways to Learn about Cells, Bones, Muscles, and Joints
Michelle O'Brien Palmer

Sixty hands-on games, experiments, and activities show what the cells of an orange look like, how our spines are constructed, how our knees and elbows work, and much more.

ages 7–12
ISBN-13: 978-1-55652-367-0
ISBN-1o: 1-55652-367-X
152 pages, paper, $14.95

Sandbox Scientist
Real Science Activities for Little Kids
Michael E. Ross
Illustrated by Mary Anne Lloyd
Parents, teachers, and day-care leaders learn to assemble "Explorer Kits" that will send kids off on their own investigations, in groups or individually, with a minimum of adult intervention.
ages 2–8
ISBN-13: 978-1-55652-248-2
ISBN-10: 1-55652-248-7
208 pages, paper, $12.95

Sense-Abilities
Fun Ways to Explore the Senses for Children 4 to 8
Michelle O'Brien-Palmer
Dozens of fun and original science activities that explore taste, touch, sight, smell, and hearing.
ISBN-13: 978-1-55652-327-4
ISBN-10: 1-55652-327-0
176 pages, paper, $14.95